cartooning for kids!
Crazy, Zany
cartoon characters

By Dave Garbot

Welcome! Drawing crazy, zany cartoon characters is a lot of fun! There is no right or wrong way to draw them. It's all up to you and your imagination!

This library edition published in 2015 by Walter Foster Jr.,
an imprint of Quarto Publishing Group USA Inc.
3 Wrigley, Suite A
Irvine, CA 92618

Distributed in the United States and Canada by
Lerner Publisher Services
241 First Avenue North
Minneapolis, MN 55401 U.S.A.
www.lernerbooks.com

First Library Edition

Library of Congress Cataloging-in-Publication Data

Garbot, Dave.
   Crazy, zany cartoon characters / by Dave Garbot. -- First Library Edition.
      pages cm. -- (Cartooning for kids!)
   ISBN 978-1-939581-47-1
1. Cartoon characters--Juvenile literature. 2. Drawing--Technique--Juvenile literature. I. Title.
   NC1764.G37 2014
   741.5'1--dc23

                                                                                        2014017646

062015
18882

9 8 7 6 5 4 3 2 1

Table of Contents

What You Will Need...

crayons

colored pencils

markers

pencil

eraser

drawing paper

Don't be afraid to draw. You can always erase!

Getting Started

Before we get this show on the road,
here is an important tip:
When you draw crazy, happy, and
zany characters, it's important to
smile and have fun! If you're happy, your
drawing will look happy too!
Smile big, grab your pencil and paper,
and let's start drawing!

Funny Faces

Let's start out with a few basics. Here are a few facial features we will use on our crazy, zany characters.

Eyes

Eyes can be goofy, sleepy, and mysterious (yikes!). They can be different sizes or even just simple dots.

Noses

Noses, beaks, snouts, and schnozzes can be different shapes too.

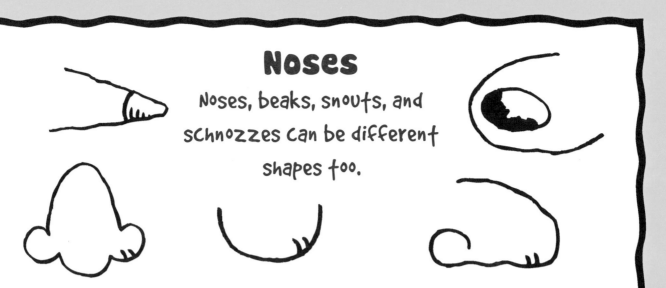

Mouths

Mouths can be a simple squiggle; an unhappy frown; or a great, big cheesy grin!

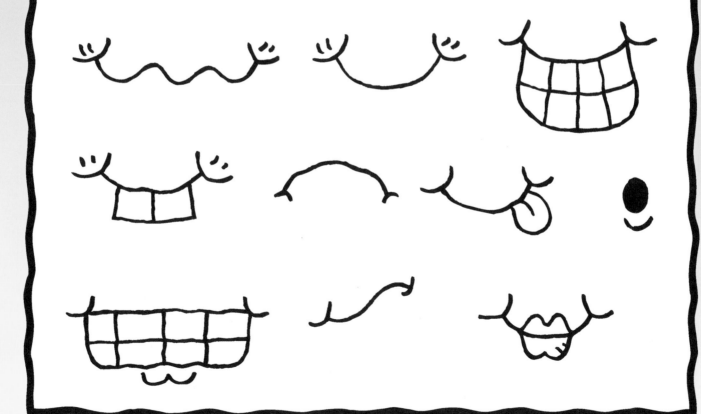

Head Shapes

Here are some basic head shapes.
We'll use some of these examples later.

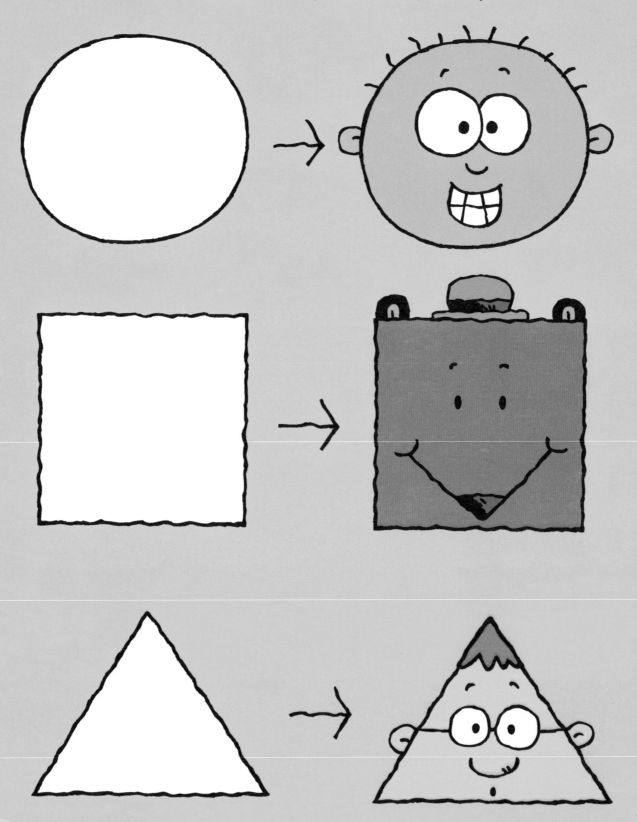

Accessories

crazy, zany
characters use lots
of accessories.
Here are a few ideas
to keep in mind
as you draw.

Expressions

Expressions can tell a lot about our characters and how they feel. They are usually pretty happy, but maybe the character you draw is tired, surprised, or extra excited! You can use facial expressions and gestures to help express emotions and personality.

Happy

Sick

Confused

Worried

Amused

Crazy Creatures

In this section you will learn how to draw a variety of crazy creatures. Some are animals you see every day, such as a dog, a squirrel, or a bird. But this group also has a goofy dino and even an alien from outer space! (I don't think you see those in your neighborhood too often.)

Try to experiment with how you add color to your drawings and which accessories you choose. A funny hat, glasses, an umbrella, or even a cute little purse can make these creatures look more interesting and silly. Above all, have fun and use your imagination!

Squirrelly Sam

Let's draw our first character by starting with a simple shape. When you're done, can you give Sam a hat or a pair of glasses?

15

Big Guppy

This big guppy has spots, but maybe you can think of something else to make your fishy look different. How about stars, swirls, or even stripes?

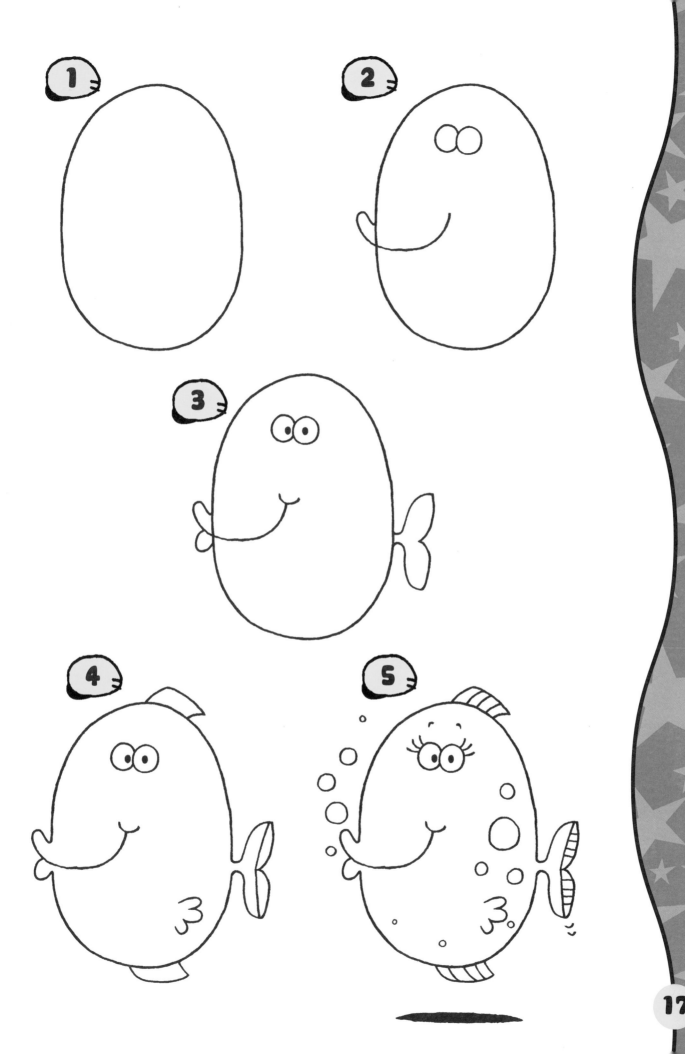

17

Tweeter Bird

Tweeter has his eyes closed in this drawing.
Can you change that? Choose a pair of eyes from page 6
to help this bird see where he's going!

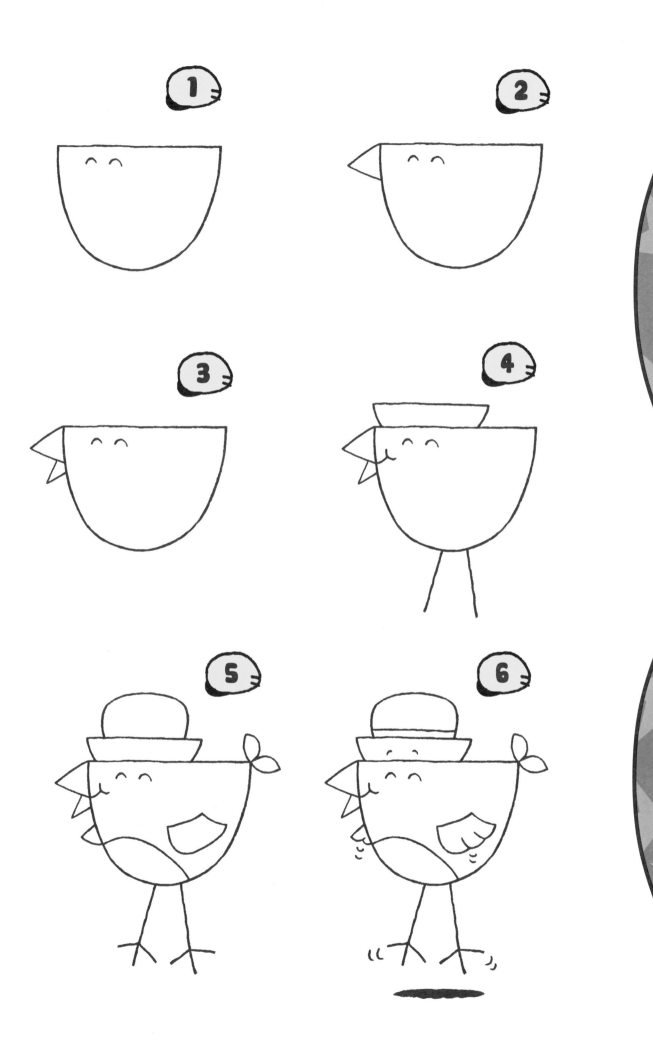

Alien Bob

Bob has four eyes in this drawing.
Can you give him 6 or even 7?

Happy Pup

This is one happy pooch!
Follow these steps and draw one for yourself.

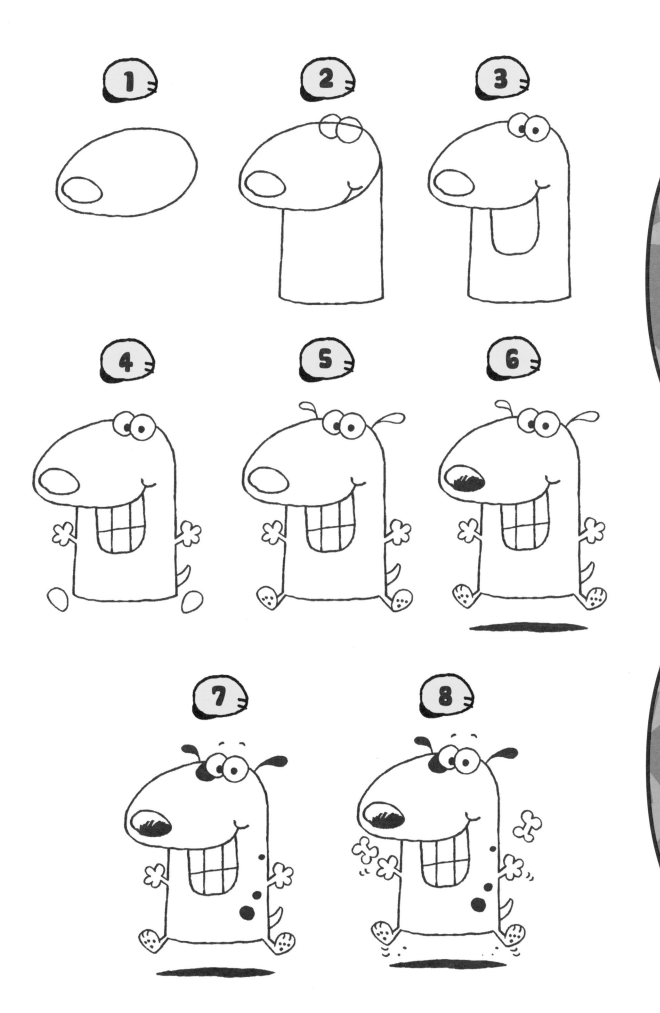

23

Smiley Dino

This smiley dino is pretty cool, but maybe he could use a hat?
Go back to the Accessories section on page 9 if you need an idea.

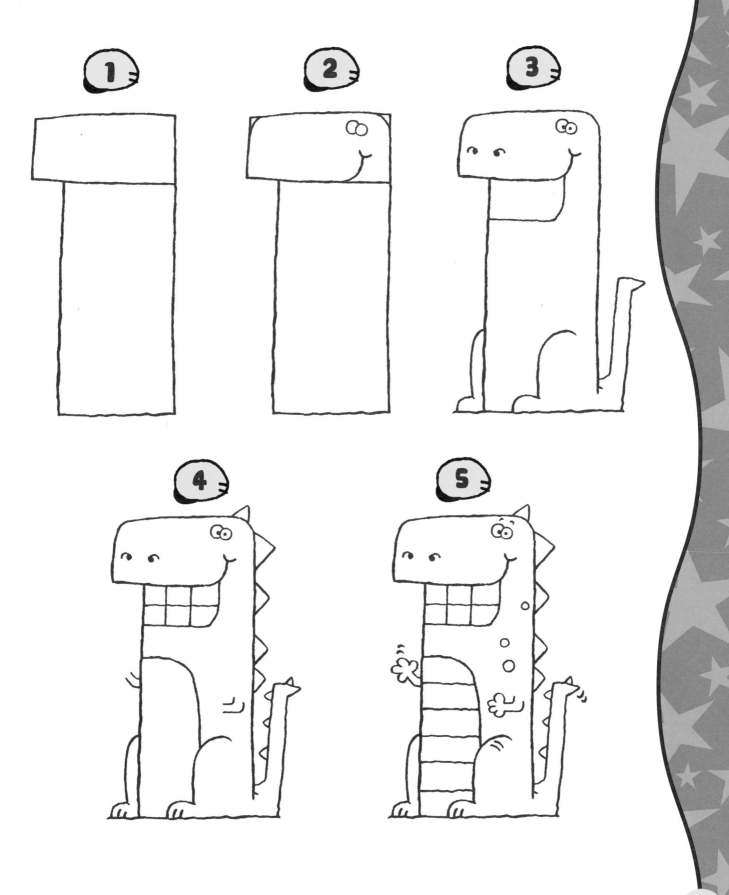

25

Henry the Horse

Henry looks a little crazy with his
spots and colors. Do you think he needs a hat,
shoes, or maybe even a tie? Think of things you
can add, or erase, to make him look different!

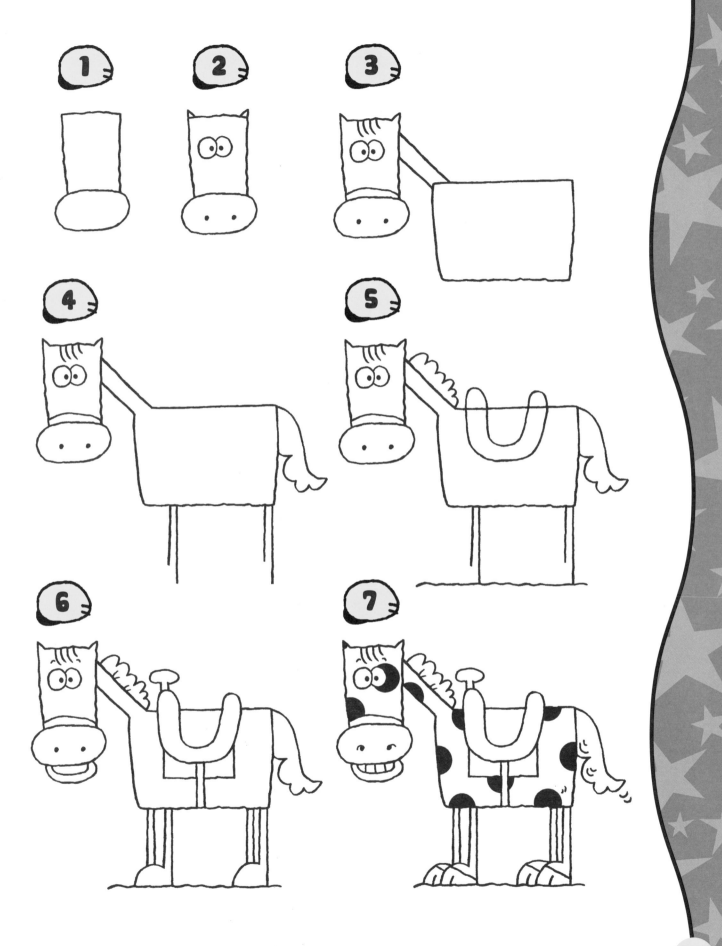

Anthropomorphic Animals

Now there's a funny word... It means animals or objects that
act or look like people! Zany characters do this often.
In this section we'll draw funny anthropomorphic characters.
Have you ever seen a real bear wear a tie? I didn't think so.

Square Head Bear

This bear wears a tie to work every day, but all you need to draw him are simple shapes. Follow the steps on the opposite page to draw Square Head Bear.

Groovy Gator

This groovy guy already looks pretty cool, but maybe you can give him a hat too. How about a sombrero?

Cool Deer

Oh, deer! He's pretty cool with those shades, but let's take the glasses off so we can see his eyes. Go back to page 6 and choose a pair of eyes to give this deer a new "look."

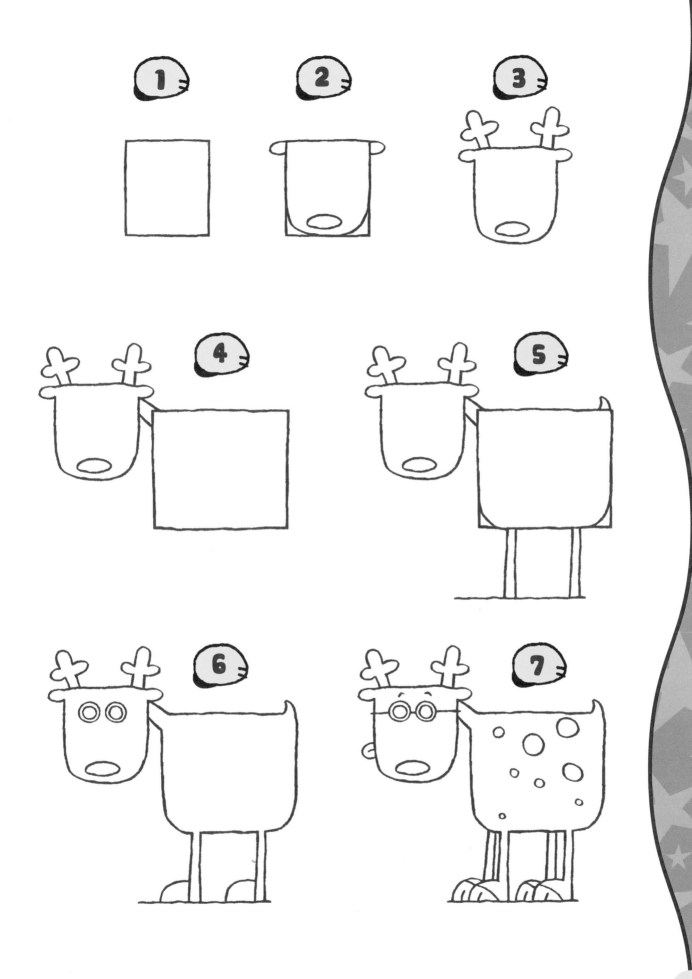

Juggles the Raccoon

Nice work, Juggles, but what else can you juggle?
Balls, carrots...what do you think? Be creative and
have fun with it!

37

Perky Penguin

The thing about penguins is that you always seem to see more than just one! After you draw this penguin, can you use different accessories and colors to create some friends to keep him company?

Flying Pig

Have you ever heard the expression "That will happen when pigs fly?" Here's your chance to make it come true! Pigs don't like to fly alone, either. Make sure to draw more than one on your page!

Ellie the Elephant

A purple elephant...really? Anything is possible with crazy, zany characters! For more fun, give Ellie some polka dots or different colors.

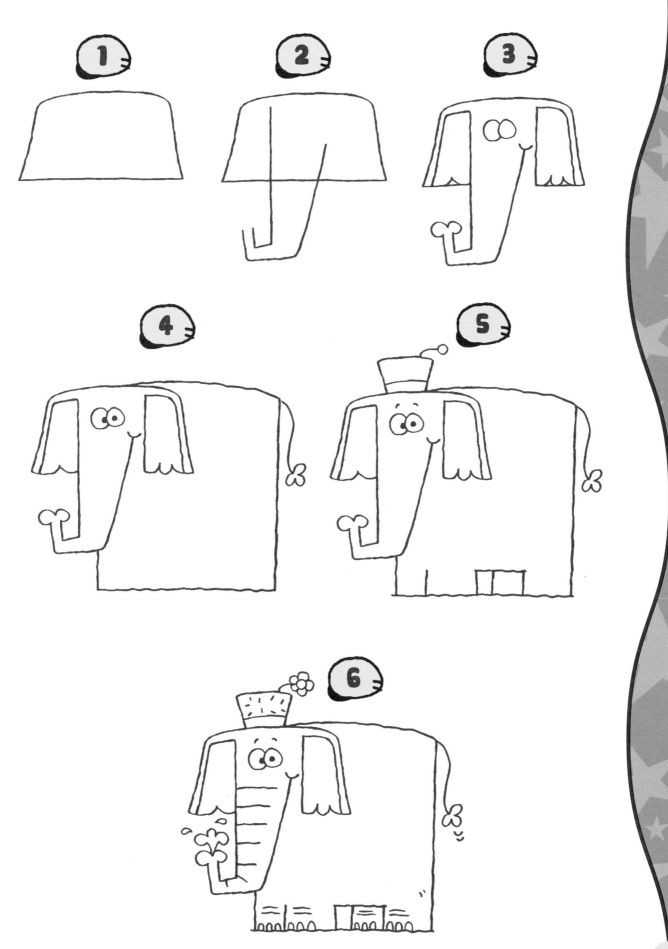

Cow & Friend

Our cow has a small bird sitting with him, but maybe
you'd like to change that to another type of friend.
How about one of the characters we've already drawn instead?
Maybe a small penguin or a raccoon?!

45

People & Professions

Sometimes you will draw a character who has a special job or something in their personality that makes them unique. Your character might be a chef, an astronaut, a firefighter, or even a zookeeper! This is when accessories really come in handy. A special hat, a uniform, or an object can easily show who your character is or what kind of job it does. In this section we'll "dress up" our friends a bit by adding more accessories—and extra fun!

Pizza Bear

Right now this bear is driving a pizza car, but maybe you can think of something else for him to deliver. Go back to page 9 for more ideas. How about a carrot delivery mobile or a banana bus?

49

Chef Morty

This birthday cake looks delicious, but wouldn't it be fun to switch it out for something silly? Oops... sorry, chef!

Betty Ballerina

Betty is a fancy dancer. Maybe you would like her to have a different colored outfit or a new hairstyle?

53

Bobby Baseball

Start with the simple shapes shown on the opposite page and before you know it, you will have Bobby stealing second base!

55

Bird Lady

We know this is the "bird lady" because of the silly birdies in her hat. But what if the birds flew away? What would you add in their place?

57

Zookeeper

This Zookeeper has her hands full with snakes—Yikes! What can you do to make your drawing different from the example?

ZOO

Cowboy

How would this cowboy look if you changed his hat?
(Maybe a little crazy and zany!)
Go back to page 9 if you need an idea for
our friend from the wild, wild west.

Firefighter Fred

Fred is pretty happy in this drawing.
Can you change his expression to something else?

About the Author

Dave Garbot is a professional illustrator and has been drawing for as long as he can remember. He is frequently called on to create his characters for children's books and other publications. Dave always has a sketchbook with him and gets many of his ideas from the things he observes every day, as well as from lots of colorful childhood memories. Although he admits that creating characters brings him personal enjoyment, making his audience smile, feel good, and maybe even giggle is what really makes his day.